USBORNE FIRST READING
Level Three

For more titles in this series go to
www.usborne.com

Owls

Sarah Courtauld

Illustrated by Lorna Hussey

Reading Consultant: Alison Kelly
Roehampton University

In the night,
all is quiet.

Far away, a pale
shape appears.

An owl flies by on
silent wings.

He lands on a branch
and looks around.

Owls can see in the dark
with their big, round eyes.

And they can turn
their heads almost all
the way around.

5

Owls can hear very
well, too.

This owl can hear a
fox creeping along the
ground...

...a bat flitting through
the sky...

...and even a tiny twig
falling out of a tree.

7

The owl
sits still and
listens hard.

He hears a pitter patter on
the ground.

Pitter
Patter

He dives down,

grabs a mouse in his claws,
and flies off.

He lands on a tree
branch and swallows
the mouse in one gulp.

Gulp!

Then...

Krrkkkk

Krrrr

Krrr

Krrkkkugghhh!

A furry ball flies
out of his mouth.

Inside it are all the bits the
owl doesn't want.

Owls come in all shapes
and sizes, and they live all
over the world.

Pels owls live by
rivers and hunt for fish.

Eagle owls live in
forests and catch rabbits.

15

And snowy owls live high
up on mountains.

They pounce on
voles and mice.

Almost all owls hunt at night. Each owl likes its own space to hunt in.

Pip pip pip

So owls call out to keep other owls away. Different owls have different calls.

The spotted
owlet shrieks.

The barn owl cries.

Cheevak

Ee–uuuu

The pygmy owl sings.

Hu hu hu hu

Ke-aaa

And the rusty barred
owl screeches.

21

In the daytime,
owls hide.

They stay
perfectly still.

They are very
hard to spot.
How many can
you see?

Every year in spring, owls
find a partner.

Twit

A male owl calls
to a female owl.

She calls back and comes
to find him.

Twooooooo

Next they make a nest.
Some owls nest
in holes in trees.

Some owls nest
in rabbit burrows.

This tiny elf owl nests
inside a big spiky plant.

Inside her nest, the female owl lays three round, white eggs.

She sits on the eggs
to keep them warm.

29

After a few weeks, the
eggs hatch.

Three baby owls are born.

They stay in the nest with
their mother.

Their father hunts and
brings back food.

33

Then, the mother goes hunting too. The baby owls start to explore their nest...

...until their mother comes
back with a tasty snack.

Day by day, the baby owls grow. Soon, they want to know what lies beyond their nest.

One by one,
they climb outside.

They shuffle along
the branches.

One baby owl flaps
her wings.

She jumps off the
branch and...

Plonk!

She tries
again...

and again...

and again...

until...

she can fly!

At last, all the
baby owls can fly.

They learn to hunt for their own food.

At the end of the summer,
the baby owls leave their nest
for the last time.

One by one, they take off
and fly away.

45

Owl facts

 A barn owl can see 50 times better than a human in the dark.

 Owls can turn their heads 280 degrees.

 Owls in cold places have feathers all over their feet to keep warm.

 Owls have two toes pointing to the front and two toes pointing to the back. This helps them catch their prey.

Index

Owl websites

You can find out more about owls by
going to the Usborne Quicklinks
Website www.usborne-quicklinks.com
and typing in the keywords "first
reading owls". Then click on the link
for the website you want to visit.

Internet Guidelines
The recommended websites are regularly reviewed
and updated but, please note, Usborne Publishing is
not responsible for the content of any website other
than its own. We recommend that young children
are supervised while on the internet.

Consultant: Derek Niemann
Designed by Louise Flutter
Series editor: Lesley Sims
Series designer: Russell Punter

First published in 2009 by Usborne Publishing Ltd.,
Usborne House, 83-85 Saffron Hill, London EC1N 8RT, England.
www.usborne.com Copyright © 2009 Usborne Publishing Ltd.

USBORNE FIRST READING
Level Four